Mr. Morgan Keeps Our School Clean

Susan McCune

Rosen Real Readers

Rosen Classroom™
New York

Mr. Morgan is our janitor.

A janitor is someone who keeps a school clean.

Mr. Morgan is good at his job.

He is from Colombia.

Colombia is in South America.

He speaks Spanish and English.

Mr. Morgan cleans the school every day.
He mops the floor.
He waxes the floor, too.

He wears a uniform.
He wears it so we can recognize him.
His uniform is white.

Mr. Morgan wears gloves. They protect him from the cleaning chemicals.

Sometimes students drop things.
He helps us clean up the mess.

Mr. Morgan also fixes things.
He knows how to fix a sink.

He makes sure that
everything works.
Everyone at the school
needs Mr. Morgan.

During the winter, Mr. Morgan even shovels snow.

He's very strong!

We are so happy Mr. Morgan keeps our classroom clean!

Words to Know

janitor

shovel

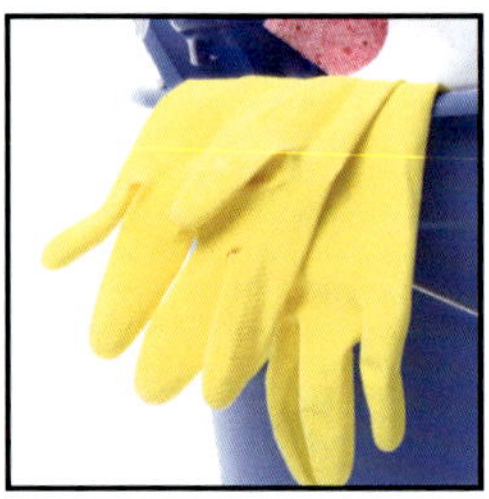

gloves

Colombia